Wizardry
OF MAN

Wizardry OF MAN

Bruce Charles Kirrage

Ordering Information:

For orders and inquiries, please contact:
1-888-404-1388
www.goldtouchpress.com
book.orders@goldtouchpress.com

Printed in the United States of America

Dedicated to

AH ML SPD LNA M M-R-D & P MEB AW & P HBAG WF
EJK JD BW & Daughter
& sons
JPCK & NGK

With special thanks to Debbie Jones, Doctors, Prisoners,
Chaplains and Prison Officers, Webb and Little, and Mr. Martin
of Norwich Prison.

Without whom this poetry would never have been written.

Index

About the Author...ix
Synopsis xiii
Messages xv

Statement..1
Death of My Father (2009) 2
How Do Future 3
Dying Flame...4
Bombay Sapphire Woman..5
From A Prison Cell (2018) 6
Jealousy...7
Red Yellow Green 8
This Straightjacket 9
Pain and Strength 10
Thumb and Forefinger 11
Fishing a Day in July 12
Tears of Love..13
Om 14
From The Shadows into Light 15
A Toyed Court 16
To Love 17
PS 18
Guilty Primes..19
To Bot...20
Elizabeth..21
Whiles 22

Further 23

Education 24

Um Tis Um Tis 25

Down The Riff of Madness 26

Bubble 29

Soul 31

Moon 32

3:2 33

Squaring the Circle 34

Lucy in the Sky, #Diamonds 35

The Gist in Us 36

To A Friend 37

To Ania 38

Loneliness 39

Mental 41

Coming Of the Bride 42

Amanda's Chuckle 43

'BTD' 44

A Litter Unjust 45

Knot Ringings 46

Electricity 47

Oz 48

Years Ago 49

Motherlove 50

Grace 51

About the Author

Bruce Charles Kirrage was born in Singapore in 1953. After moving around the world, he settled permanently in the UK in 1966. He joined the medical profession in 1973 and retired in 2010.

Since 1977, Kirrage has written poems and children's stories; other writings have been endorsed by medical consultants.

Kirrage believes in Christian principles and Zoroastrian principles. He believes God was/is the single entity that is open to the question of courage, the compassion of human or animal nature, an understanding of happiness, and an interpretation of worldly events.

Other Books:

Wizardry of Women
Wizardry of Love: Contemplation of My Soul Diagonal of My Brain
Burp, Hip, and Twist Children's Book Series

Synopsis

This is a book of poetry and prose, primarily concerning a man coming out from psychosis into reality; from a man who was once an inmate. This is based on the principle used in the first book, *"Wizardry of Women"*.

The Author believes the only aspects of life a man can have true faith in - are animals, his own children and the nature of Jesus or God (the 'innocents' in our lives if you like).

The book is an attempt to explain man's actions to man; this could go a long way to promote the characteristics of mental illness and mental wellness.

I leave it up to the readers to judge both the quality and the content.

Messages

"The motto of my old school is: 'Quae sursum sunt quaerite' - 'Seek those things which are above': do you think I don't stick by that?

There's a place in the brain that has a part for God. It's in every human being

For me I cannot watch TV when they show the pain of children suffering. It brings me to tears. I have to turn away

Animals are just as bad for me to see them suffering too

As for adults there is some hope, yet usually it's fleeting

I was betrayed I'm sure of that and that is why I'm angry and slow to trust people

I trust you best way I can

Yet of the two- Stella or me you'd put Stella first. Am I right yes?

And I wouldn't think anything of the worst of you

She keeps you on an even keel and would never leave your side

No man could promise you that and mean it

The only other true concept is God and he/she lives in our minds

Am I right?

'I don't believe in God'

That's where all the nice things come from

You do believe in art and your animals. They are your God

You just can't put it in words that's why you can deny

I'm not preaching. Others would say the same

What you love on this earth is a representation of your God

'But I don't believe in bible'

You don't have to it was written by men

And is an allegory

Yes

'This all religions are fake'

No not fake. Just a help

What you say is closer to Gods words than men

I believe that. Hence my book 'Wizardry Of Women'

It was an attempt to reach the mind of a woman

How else do men exist?

Women are the better half and the better boss

I believe that too

A matriarchal society is what this world is moving towards

Men are basically useless. They adore fighting and winning. Few women I believe see that as really relevant

Kindness is the only attribute a man can be taught otherwise he'll never learn

'Yes'"

'Statement'

I give as and all I hold dear of a good healthy love, born from
around those that is in pain
Those that have little gain, those that dies hardy,
Those that is young and weedy; I give you my mishaps to forgive.
My forgiving me of my drifting, my essence of token
Yet through this I give you yeah, forever a part called love

'Death of My Father (2009)'

Has no edge as it cast its spell
No thought unwound
It's this living in black hell
It has no fear
As it tears at the heart
Its ink lives on as wit, science and art

'How Do Future'

How do win where others fail
How does less yet be more
How to start begun before
Tell me Goddess
And will happiness be
Tell me Lord
For to let know
Willed if willing win
Now and forevermore
Yet I beguile sin
From without to within

'Dying Flame'

When the flame has died
And you've cried and cried
What is there
But a long time before death
And all of life is lived where

You were once happy
And smiles were there
Now that's gone
And you've nothing to wear
You're just nobody nowhere

The dance is a dim memory
And rings and things
Disappear luv
Was she really
The angel from above

Did the gin
Really help anything
Did the red wine
Make your heart sing

And your love was bound up
In lies and discord
Yet you know it cut my heart
Like a knife or the sword

'Bombay Sapphire Woman'

She was top rank
The rest cowing
Blacking
As to her dress
Her my kissed while standing
Now and same before
Other wonder eh grinning
Small talk as arises
Sound of living light was right
I need glasses

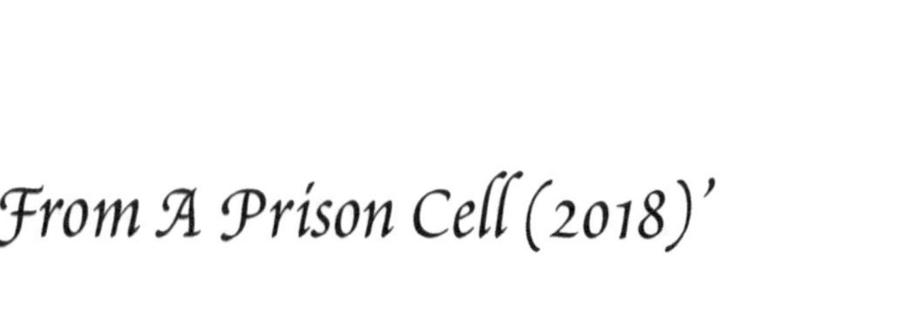

'From A Prison Cell (2018)'

The clout of prison has been clouted
While a Jesu on the cross
Had friends nearby
Yet I have no one here
Only the smell of my own fear
A fart and likely shit
Are the only ones of it
Now that my sons far away
And me a prison house not a home
Friends far away too
As I pray I call upon them and you
And life cuts so thin
It's as if a doctor are afar and not in

'Jealousy'

Her kisses with me were so sweet like wine
But she had the sting of a bee
She was an Elizabeth you see

She was a beauty to behold
No-one to me 'tis finer true
Giving a welcome just as much
Me as another too

It's been said of her a slut
As she opens her legs to a moneyed professor
I not rich enough
And left trailing behind in the rough

I the man who had loved her
And for her the daughter was
The reason to change
Me considered by them seriously deranged

As the professor surveys his beauty he had gained
Pound coins leap into her eyes
And so her love is given with flattery and lies

As the sleeping man looks such a fool
For it was the daughter's paid education she did yearn
When will elderly professor men ever learn

'Red Yellow Green'

Red yellow green
And things in between
Brown black mud
Sanctify the dead
Get it into your head

Rorty was said
Read in bed
And the rest of it
Blood sweat and tears
Sears

Gainsborough guess
Whereby invest
Through art
At and after
Pecuniary laughter

Faster cry
Why oh why
Om the present
Super-heated meet
Quick quicker seat

'This Straightjacket'

As I die from the inside
And Christmas is around about
The thought of happiness disappears
With no liquor beer or stout

And I die each day a little more
The devil in me to her reaches out
As I lay slumped in a chair
Without

Where oh where is her
From this straightjacket I be
Anyway to get there and away
Please God let me be free

'Pain and Strength'

I have cried out as I pine Martin
Cried with the pain in
Even in pining
Martin had birds all around him
He could not doubt
Polite and trim
Yet I feeling have no friends here
Though I call and shout
Even May is out
And coon uncaring
If you had known a-sparing

Between heaven and what is vexed
To not cometh between
To not there render unseen
And to the innermost side
Between love and pride
To not deal in death
Be a living star
Living and loving
We all can be as are

'Thumb and Forefinger'

Do not let me succumb
To the other fortunes of thumb
Yet linger with me always
I pray whatever
Your turquoise colour desire
For between love and the finger
Lies the boundary of my light
For you cry out a Cygnet bird yet
Nothing breaks the five fingers
I know of you to nay yore
A lie the ones before
It's not for me a starry night
I will seek only to pen that right

'Fishing a Day in July'

The fish come biting
And I sit and wonder at it
Firstly arrives one here
A small dear
There is one
And then another
For soon there is a monster
The only one
Hits me at a ton
The line hook rod broke
My head in a yoke
Lost and gone
I say to you
Good folk

'Tears of Love'

The tears of love do abound
And the heart is found
And I know my love is sound
When the only sound is the voice of one's own
Then the pillar of salt that is you
The come to me my lovely
When prior thought to be dead
The missing letters
Dart from one's head
I will fill that head
With the only love to know
Of a man who with you
Can subtly grow
The I and the he of it
Become we
Then you have the epitome of me
You are the only one
That did it for me
The whole of life
Amid a bitter-sweet tragedy
Pathos reigns
And with your namesake too
Long live all of you

'Om'

The future scream Om
The future is free
This will be
Come as the phantom
You will see
As you are
The lock and key
Funkey
Rise as a rocket
You will fit my hard and solid tree

'From The Shadows into Light'

Three men from Mars
Flying space cars
Gain again
Shape the pain
From a deep well within
Encapsulate a vase
Say when to for you
Others shoo shoo
Pictures of flowers
Desist hateful Writings
Endure the sightings
Refuel fuller gourd
And deliver a better word

'A Toyed Court'

We drag our thought up
From the gutter
Painfully at first
Yet when what rehearsed
Given our hunger and thirst
Then forthcoming ideas
Typed on
Yeah kindled
Like a fire on a hearth
Do you well
Do what's worth

Freshly burst
Seeking diligence
Not a little reticence
And resisting hardness
Lending itself to fondness
Away to the bridged port
Sought

'To Love'

I have cried with the happiness of...
How does any woman
Differentiate
And knowing me best
Yet not talked with and
Having of a countenance blessed
Teach me by enduring lesson
To never think of
Other things than love
Such that not being married
Keep me alive
When few had wished me to be
How does that lady
Yet know me so well
Yet not being with me
For many a long spell (of time)
Her never saying....
Her never speaking of.....
Yet her few words spoken are....
As a peace from afar
And I say too
Bless her

'PS'

Make a face at me
No poetry
Make an edict
Get out of town clown
Once defined
Neatly rhymed
Wronged one
Just to talk some
Forget the low down bum
Him not to come
This I pray
As I elsewhere stay

'Guilty Primes'

The doubling o'er the primes
As they run up the ladder
As sullied through the air
And yet after care
Me an anxious thought
A known as it ought

'To Bot'

Body buggered condenses
As the mind commended senses
As malleable as copper hammer
Out of drill wood brick
Begone stick
Roundabout tick
Slow down
Middle to ground
Begun from Hi
Gnashes as saying my oh my
Coming down
To that Bot net
Hope succeeds
Hope set
Expands from future knot
Hope from hope
To Skype not

'Elizabeth'

Never have I seen such hair
Radiance beyond compare
The flowing lock
Lucky me to clock
Find my watch tick-tock
To put on right there

'Whiles'

All there a while
A hopeful smile
Lives a girl
With her hair to unfurl
Across many a mile
To free me
I know I ought to
Please put me to task
Is all I ask

'Further'

The last taste moreover
Of African clover
Is barely sufficient
Indian somewhat clever
The Americanisation
Of a Romanian woman
By hand bostik
Succulent delight
And Chinese is all left over right
Yet the dreamily seemingly
Conjugation
Of the Alabaster Englishwoman
Is purposefully
The very highest height
Down doing nite

'Education'

Was it my education that makes me write
More like desperation
To earn a few bob
To yet be a knob
Or one who eschews
A life of subordination

'Um Tis Um Tis'

Um tis um tis Encephalitis then
As a child when
Fevered to 105
Barely alive
Dunk him in
Cold iced water
His heart again will begin

'Down The Riff of Madness'

Down the riff of madness
Where the devil is the lure
Where a doctor gives drugs
To where to which paranoia cure

Where authority bans by spurious means
To aid or help the love what is seems
Through the needle or tablet
The crisis addict reborn
As from a Goliath one be shorn

When the real dawn is far away
And only the blackness of hell awaits forlorn
Further drugged isolation drawn
Further no sleep
And slighted equality
By the love-drug his self so torn
As he fights to maintain stability

Give me the voice to say as I write
For I as a pill box of society
A maddening joke
With only the hope of reason to cloak

Give me an ending like this
Written around
With his last gasp
He died
He held her ecstatic
By arms her to clasp

This may be written
As I call out innocently
Her name of which I'm proud to have known
With lights burning in my soul
One for her
And one for all the others now flown

For the greyness of the matter
Is an anti-matter
In a world populated by authority
Madder than it
Where the ass of law hides it

A sumptuous act dropped
And the injection riddled too
As sleep is hindered stopped
That is as I write you

As to the asses side of heaven
The commoner prisoner patient
Up and away is driven
To a place far away
To beyond hell
As to Norwich Prison

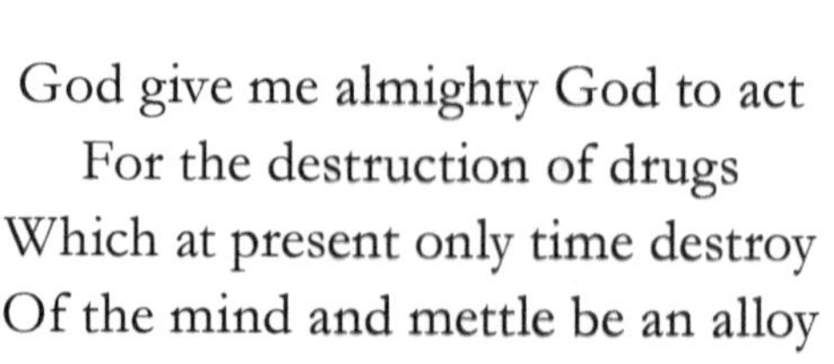

God give me almighty God to act
For the destruction of drugs
Which at present only time destroy
Of the mind and mettle be an alloy

'Tis the authorities wish
Of whom they employ
And to leave nothing behind
As blinded by love
And now grown fatter bruv'

Cherish strength
The arc of one to give
Yet I inherent write
Live to let alive be live

'Bubble'

When life is all bubble
And goals less trouble
Beware of love's curse
The hidden hand of desire

It comes as it does
Not even a shaman or any human
Does it not breach to teach

And the healing hand
Seems impossible you understand
Then one knows
A timely desire

Odds and even numbers
Letters scramble into mind
The one of it
And why of it

And disappear before the wise
Every imaginable
Combination of goodly
Passes before the eyes

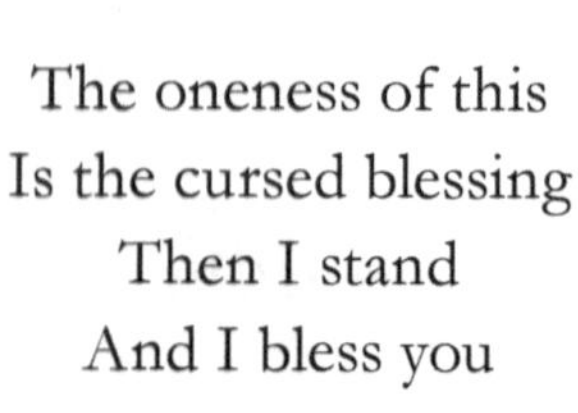

The oneness of this
Is the cursed blessing
Then I stand
And I bless you

This life
This newer life
Unprepossessing and unhindered by greed

For others are in some way
The luckier ones
And therefore and I say it done
God bless everyone

As tear comes to eye
And pain by that yet
Some have yet to gain
To discover

As yet the thrust of this as doing
Good how does
Yet does come of it

That as does
And that forever
Was and lovingly should be
You all and me

'Soul'

Only if you have hope in your soul
Can you be totally whole
Sang the man from the moon
Who played to you a happier tune

'Moon'

There once was a man from the moon
Who played everyone a happier tune
It wasn't the music though that was good too
It was the meaning behind the words
That we could all do

'3:2'

Three into two will go
I know
Look at a chair and double settee
Space in between with a side-table or two
First chair from right to
Then side-table
Then settee
Then the last side-table to do

'Squaring the Circle'

The above is simple you see
Use a bit of maths you
Can know what to do
Apply Calculus to
The area under the curve
Is the answer for you

'Lucy in the Sky, #Diamonds'

Said I to the poet in the sky
True love aye
I fancy her hair not cropped
A just digest
As the Haliborange pill
Father you knew no ill

Curse the hides
Who seek the shoot up
So to speak

I find her pecked
Known to worry no one
Between he too
You me as goodly
An innocent neck marked you

'The Gist in Us'

And others be
The gist in all of us
This thinks the right words
Cursing with all swords
Yet love her madly more
More than forever....owe
And I cry with the suffering
And wishing time itself on in
Could remonstrate within
This remorseless finding
For as unitary kindling

'To A Friend'

The love of a friend
Should always be bourne in mind
It is something better
Than an acquaintance
Though a lived in humanity
Has justly designed
An arrangement and nicely augmented
Can bring a kind of peace
Which seemingly trusts to give
Comfort beyond yet leased

'To Ania'

I want for little Ania
To be comforted from near and afar
And held by someone
Loved by night and day
Would be the kindest of things done I say
Until and whenever
That special day arrives for her again
I'll play my trade
As forever with hand and pen

'Loneliness'

And only
When you are lonely
And giving out pathetically
When another's name
Cannot be driven away such
When the blindness hurts so much

'Tis beyond
When life's force
Is driving one into the ground
When the past has gone
And you feel the solitariness of one

When living justice and peace
Push one into the ground
When self attaches to no one
When all the above
Cries out in you
And is let upon

Then you have the itinerary of it
You are as you stand move or sit
And living is as life comes undone
And before as a simpleton

A baby as with croup
Alone one two or three
Or as a group
You are shut out

In knowing that the going
Is no longer open
And she does beckon upon
And one's body does ache
And life is very tired of you

Then the lonesome of one
Amidst the few moreover
We become the dove
With angst from below and above

'Mental'

Acuphase was given
As a truck driven
Through a building
By a female nurse
A syringe wielding
For compliance sake
I was forced to take

I not thankful unyielding
They without feeling
As I later tore down a fire door
To let a disabled wheelchair in for

Looked down upon from out to within
As the doctor glanced in
He said for the police and
Prison to be led
I had been assessed

'Coming Of the Bride'

It's the coming of the bride
And the happening inside
It's the breaking in two
Of the stick we once knew
It's the hammer-fist duke
There I contemplate to puke
What is this then to be
Said the birds to the bee

'Amanda's Chuckle'

This is a little poem for Amanda
Whose chuckle on the phone
Appears a little kinder
Long may her chuckle be lasting
Over the holiday and forever more
As my thoughts turn to God
And the happenings before

'BTD'

The pain hones in
Tearing through my brain
God gives no quarter
Has everything
Has everything to gain
Looks neither right nor left
Sears all as to defy all odds
Begat nothing
Of the sods that cling
Bugger The Dope
All is given up
Up for hope....

'A Litter Unjust'

Finding perchance a litter unjust
As up to one percent
If me such thing need reminded
What should and could not be spent
Yours truly reminded from thirty-eight to completing Monday to
Sunday
To following Friday
God willing to those few days to go
From herein now
Great thankful allow

'Knot Ringings'

He has wronged
Where wrong should not be hidden
To hide where hide should not be hidden
To create injustice by not any other name
To shed blame where blame is not due
And by that task
Will be unmasked yet
For I will never forget
That man without a name
Not me and not the same
I gave HER my 'ring thing'
HER has my everything
I gave HER my heart
HER knew me from start
HER knew as yet horse before cart
I gave HER little importude
Things consciously glued
Yeah mine too
For as once may have been said
Her guile and quest true
For me just and picturesque
And sobriety 'normaility'
Henceforth 'sendendipitously'

'Electricity'

The spoon is in the roll
The knife is in the cup
And the fork is on the plate
A subsidizing bowl for the many
An impudence between lips
And the spoon is on a roll
A slip up between doves
And the cup encircles the knife
The then Pacific rimmed plates
Creates from a love above
The bowlfuls for the many states

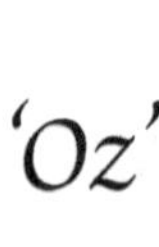

'Oz'

Oz tried and Oz denied
The PCSCREW lost his temper
So out with through window with screw
Here to do

'Years Ago'

A brown elsewhere came
Forever denied by me now
Shits comfortably no more
See and never a fun-key so pissed
Is he on his window ledge -
and thinking he on the thinnest of edge

'Motherlove'

I cry with the happiness of
How does a woman who knows me best
Yet not talked with and having of a countenance blessed
Teach me an enduring lesson
Two never think of another with any act
Such that and (not) married
Yet keep me alive
When few at time wish me so to be
How does a lady
Know me so well
Yet not be with me physically
For many a long spell of time
HER never saying or speak long to me
Out loud of love
Yet her past few words spoken are

'Grace'

It is to Grace I give you this poem
For all by your hand to know 'em
A restful sleep to you and them
By favour and to you fortune
And by favour to others in tune